T011492

WELCOME TO THE CAPTIVATING WORLD OF
"BIBLICAL BLACK LOVE"
A COLORING JOURNEY THROUGH COUPLES
IN THE BIBLE!"

EMBARK ON AN ENCHANTING ADVENTURE
THROUGH TIME AND FAITH AS WE DELVE
INTO THE REMARKABLE STORIES OF
14 EXTRAORDINARY COUPLES FROM
THE SACRED SCRIPTURES.

BIBLICAL BLACK LOVE

AN ADULT COLORING BOOK

APRIL LA'PREZZ

authorHOUSE

author**HOUSE**°

Published by AuthorHouse 12/20/2023

Print information available on the last page.

ISBN: 979-8-8230-1894-4 (sc)

This book is printed on acid-free paper.

Certain stock imagery © Getty Images.

Any people depicted in stock imagery provided by Getty Images are models,
and such images are being used for illustrative purposes only.

Because of the dynamic nature of the Internet, any web addresses or links contained in this book may have changed
since publication and may no longer be valid. The views expressed in this work are solely those of the author and do not
necessarily reflect the views of the publisher, and the publisher hereby disclaims any responsibility for them.

AuthorHouse™
1663 Liberty Drive
Bloomington, IN 47403
www.authorhouse.com
Phone: 833-262-8899

No part of this book may be reproduced, stored in a retrieval system, or transmitted
by any means without the written permission of the author.

© 2023 April La'Prezz. All rights reserved.

To my beloved parents, Rick and Tanja,
Your unwavering love and support have been the cornerstone of my
life's journey. From the very beginning, you instilled in me a profound
appreciation for our culture, our spirituality, and the power of love.
This coloring book, "Biblical Black Love," is a reflection of the values
you've imparted and the heritage you've cultivated within our family. It
is dedicated to you both with profound gratitude for the foundation
you've provided and the love that continues to guide my path. May the
pages of this book resonate with the love and strength you've shown me
throughout my life.

With all my love,
April
"Bunt/April-Mae"

21 BIBLICAL COUPLES

ADAM & EVE

IN THE BEGINNING, THERE WAS ADAM AND EVE, THE VERY FIRST COUPLE TO GRACE THE EARTH. THEIRS IS A STORY OF INNOCENCE, CURIOSITY, AND THE FATEFUL CHOICE THAT FOREVER CHANGED HUMANITY'S DESTINY.

COLOR THE PAGES WITH HUES OF WONDER AS YOU DEPICT THE LUSH GARDEN OF EDEN, WHERE ADAM AND EVE REVELED IN GOD'S BOUNTIFUL CREATION. LET THEIR LOVE RADIATE THROUGH EVERY STROKE, AS THEY DISCOVERED THE JOYS OF COMPANIONSHIP, EXPLORING THE VAST BEAUTY AROUND THEM HAND IN HAND.

GENESIS 2:18 (NIV)

"THEN THE LORD GOD SAID, "IT IS NOT GOOD FOR THE MAN TO BE ALONE; I WILL MAKE HIM A HELPER SUITABLE FOR HIM."

ABRAHAM & SARAH

STEP INTO THE FASCINATING WORLD OF
ABRAHAM AND SARAH, A COUPLE WHOSE
UNWAVERING FAITH AND UNYIELDING LOVE
SHAPED THE COURSE OF HISTORY. THEIRS IS A
TALE OF EXTRAORDINARY JOURNEYS,
MIRACULOUS PROMISES, AND THE FULFILLMENT
OF DREAMS AGAINST ALL ODDS.

WITH YOUR COLORING TOOLS IN HAND, BRING
TO LIFE THE VAST LANDSCAPES OF ANCIENT
MESOPOTAMIA, WHERE ABRAHAM AND SARAH
FIRST HEARD THE DIVINE CALL. LET THE
COLORS OF THE DESERT SANDS REFLECT THEIR
UNWAVERING DETERMINATION AS THEY LEFT
BEHIND THEIR HOMELAND, EMBARKING ON A
PERILOUS JOURNEY GUIDED SOLELY BY
THEIR FAITH.

GENESIS 21:12(NIV)

"BUT GOD SAID TO ABRAHAM, "DO NOT LET
IT BE DISPLEASING IN YOUR SIGHT
BECAUSE OF A LAD OR BECAUSE OF YOUR
BONDWOMAN. WHATEVER SARAH HAS SAID
TO YOU, LISTEN TO HER VOICE, FOR IN
ISAAC YOUR SEED SHALL BE CALLED."

ISAAC & REBEKAH

STEP INTO THE ENCHANTING WORLD OF ISAAC AND REBEKAH, A COUPLE WHOSE STORY RESONATES WITH TENDER ROMANCE, DIVINE PROVIDENCE, AND THE POWER OF A LOVE THAT SURPASSES TIME. THEIRS IS A TALE THAT WEAVES TOGETHER DESTINY, DEVOTION, AND THE BEAUTY OF A LOVE THAT BLOOMED IN THE ANCIENT LAND OF CANAAN.

AS YOU HOLD YOUR COLORING TOOLS, LET THE PAGES COME ALIVE AND TRANSPORT YOURSELF TO THE BUSTLING MARKETPLACE WHERE ISAAC'S HEART SKIPPED A BEAT UPON GLIMPSING THE RADIANT REBEKAH. WITH EACH STROKE, CAPTURE THE SPARK OF RECOGNITION THAT IGNITED THEIR SOULS, FOREVER INTERTWINING THEIR PATHS.

GENESIS 24:67 (NIV)

"AND ISAAC BROUGHT REBEKAH INTO HIS MOTHER SARAH'S TENT, AND SHE BECAME HIS WIFE. HE LOVED HER DEEPLY"

BOAZ & RUTH

ENTER THE ENCHANTING WORLD OF BOAZ AND
RUTH, A COUPLE WHOSE LOVE STORY
TRANSCENDS BOUNDARIES, RESTORES HOPE,
AND EXEMPLIFIES THE POWER OF KINDNESS
AND LOYALTY. THEIR TALE, SET AGAINST THE
BACKDROP OF ANCIENT BETHLEHEM, WEAVES
TOGETHER THEMES OF REDEMPTION, FAITH,
AND THE TRANSFORMATIVE NATURE OF LOVE.

AS YOU PICK UP YOUR COLORING TOOLS,
ENVISION THE ROLLING HILLS OF BETHLEHEM,
PAINTED WITH THE VIBRANT COLORS OF
HARVEST. FEEL THE GENTLE BREEZE RUSTLING
THROUGH THE FIELDS AS YOU EMBARK ON A
JOURNEY THAT WILL FOREVER CHANGE THE
LIVES OF BOAZ AND RUTH.

RUTH 1: 16-17 (NIV)

"BUT RUTH SAID, "DO NOT URGE ME TO LEAVE YOU OR
TO RETURN FROM FOLLOWING YOU. FOR WHERE YOU
GO I WILL GO, AND WHERE YOU LODGE I WILL LODGE.
YOUR PEOPLE SHALL BE MY PEOPLE, AND YOUR GOD MY
GOD. WHERE YOU DIE I WILL DIE, AND THERE WILL I BE
BURIED. MAY THE LORD DO SO TO ME AND MORE ALSO
IF ANYTHING BUT DEATH PARTS ME FROM YOU."

AQUILA & PRISCILLA

STEP INTO THE REMARKABLE WORLD OF
AGRIPA AND PRISCILLA, A COUPLE WHOSE
PARTNERSHIP EXEMPLIFIES INTELLECTUAL
PROWESS, UNWAVERING FAITH, AND A
SHARED PASSION FOR SPREADING THE
TEACHINGS OF CHRIST. THEIRS IS A STORY
THAT UNFOLDS AGAINST THE BACKDROP OF
EARLY CHRISTIAN HISTORY, LEAVING AN
INDELIBLE MARK ON THE DEVELOPMENT OF
THE EARLY CHURCH.

AS YOU GRASP YOUR COLORING TOOLS,
TRANSPORT YOURSELF TO THE BUSTLING
CITY OF ROME, WHERE AGRIPA AND
PRISCILLA'S LIVES INTERTWINED WITH THE
RICH TAPESTRY OF THE APOSTOLIC ERA. LET
YOUR COLORS MIRROR THE VIBRANT
ENERGY OF THEIR INTELLECTUAL PURSUITS,
REFLECTING THE WISDOM AND DEPTH OF
THEIR SHARED KNOWLEDGE.

ROMANS 16:3 (NIV)

"GREET PRISCILLA AND AQUILA,
MY CO-WORKERS IN CHRIST JESUS".

JOSEPH & MARY

STEP INTO THE SACRED STORY OF JOSEPH
AND MARY, A COUPLE WHOSE LIVES WERE
INTERTWINED WITH DIVINE PURPOSE AND
ENTRUSTED WITH THE EXTRAORDINARY
TASK OF RAISING THE SON OF GOD. THEIRS
IS A TALE THAT SPANS THE REALMS OF
HUMILITY, FAITH, AND UNCONDITIONAL
LOVE, FOREVER ETCHED IN THE ANNALS OF
HUMAN HISTORY.

AS YOU HOLD YOUR COLORING TOOLS,
TRANSPORT YOURSELF TO THE HUMBLE
TOWN OF NAZARETH. FEEL THE WARMTH OF
THE SETTING SUN CASTING A GENTLE GLOW
UPON JOSEPH, A RIGHTEOUS AND
COMPASSIONATE MAN, AS HE MEETS MARY,
A YOUNG WOMAN OF GRACE AND PURITY.
LET YOUR COLORS CAPTURE THE SPARK OF
LOVE THAT IGNITED WITHIN THEIR HEARTS,
DESPITE THE MYSTERIES AND
UNCERTAINTIES THAT LAY AHEAD.

MATTHEW 1:24 (NIV)

"WHEN JOSEPH WOKE UP, HE DID WHAT
THE ANGEL OF THE LORD HAD
COMMANDED HIM AND TOOK MARY HOME
AS HIS WIFE."

DAVID & ABIGAIL

STEP INTO THE CAPTIVATING WORLD OF DAVID AND ABIGAIL, A COUPLE WHOSE STORY WEAVES TOGETHER BRAVERY, WISDOM, AND THE POWER OF RIGHTEOUSNESS. THEIR TALE, SET AGAINST THE BACKDROP OF ANCIENT ISRAEL, PAINTS A VIVID PICTURE OF COURAGE, DIPLOMACY, AND THE TRANSFORMATIVE IMPACT OF A VIRTUOUS HEART.

WITH YOUR COLORING TOOLS IN HAND, ENVISION THE RUGGED LANDSCAPES OF ANCIENT JUDAH. FEEL THE WARM SUN ON YOUR SKIN AS YOU IMMERSE YOURSELF IN THE NARRATIVE OF DAVID, A YOUNG SHEPHERD DESTINED TO BECOME A LEGENDARY KING, AND ABIGAIL, A WOMAN OF REMARKABLE BEAUTY AND INTELLIGENCE.

1SAMUEL 25: 32-33 (NIV)

"THEN DAVID SAID TO ABIGAIL, "BLESSED IS THE LORD GOD OF ISRAEL, WHO SENT YOU THIS DAY TO MEET ME! AND BLESSED IS YOUR ADVICE AND BLESSED ARE YOU BECAUSE YOU HAVE KEPT ME THIS DAY FROM COMING TO BLOODSHED AND FROM AVENGING MYSELF WITH MY OWN HAND".

MOSES & ZIPPORAH

STEP INTO THE AWE-INSPIRING WORLD OF MOSES AND ZIPPORAH, A COUPLE WHOSE LOVE STORY UNFOLDS AMIDST THE GRANDEUR OF MIRACLES, LIBERATION, AND THE PURSUIT OF DESTINY. THEIRS IS A TALE OF RESILIENCE, FAITH, AND THE TRANSFORMATIVE POWER OF LOVE THAT TRANSCENDS BOUNDARIES.

WITH YOUR COLORING TOOLS IN HAND, IMMERSE YOURSELF IN THE ANCIENT LANDSCAPES OF EGYPT AND THE VAST WILDERNESS. FEEL THE WARMTH OF THE DESERT SUN AS YOU EMBARK ON A JOURNEY THAT WILL SHAPE THE COURSE OF HISTORY.

EXODUS 2: 20-21 (NIV)

"HE SAID TO HIS DAUGHTERS, "SO WHERE IS HE? WHY IN THE WORLD DID YOU LEAVE THE MAN? CALL HIM, SO THAT HE MAY EAT A MEAL WITH US." MOSES AGREED TO STAY WITH THE MAN, AND HE GAVE HIS DAUGHTER ZIPPORAH TO MOSES IN MARRIAGE".

ZACHARIAS & ELIZABETH

ENTER THE ENCHANTING WORLD OF ZACHARIAS AND ELIZABETH, A COUPLE WHOSE LIVES WERE TOUCHED BY DIVINE INTERVENTION AND BLESSED WITH THE MIRACULOUS GIFT OF JOHN THE BAPTIST. THEIR STORY IS ONE OF UNWAVERING FAITH, PERSEVERANCE, AND THE FULFILLMENT OF GOD'S PROMISES.

AS YOU TAKE HOLD OF YOUR COLORING TOOLS, IMAGINE THE PEACEFUL SURROUNDINGS OF THE COUNTRY OF JUDEA. FEEL THE GENTLE BREEZE RUSTLING THROUGH THE OLIVE TREES AS YOU IMMERSE YOURSELF IN THE NARRATIVE OF ZACHARIAS, A DEVOTED PRIEST, AND ELIZABETH, A WOMAN OF DEEP FAITH AND RIGHTEOUSNESS.

LUKE 1: 6 (NIV)

"ZECHARIAH AND ELIZABETH WERE BOTH GOOD PEOPLE WHO PLEASED GOD. THEY DID EVERYTHING THE LORD COMMANDED, ALWAYS FOLLOWING HIS INSTRUCTIONS COMPLETELY".

AMRAM & JOCABETH

ENTER THE CAPTIVATING WORLD OF ARAM AND JOCABETH, A COUPLE WHOSE LIVES WERE MARKED BY EXTRAORDINARY COURAGE, FAITH, AND A DEEP COMMITMENT TO PROTECTING THEIR SON, MOSES. THEIR STORY IS ONE OF LOVE, SACRIFICE, AND THE INDOMITABLE SPIRIT OF A MOTHER'S HEART.

AS YOU PICK UP YOUR COLORING TOOLS, TRANSPORT YOURSELF TO THE ANCIENT LAND OF EGYPT, WHERE THE HEBREW PEOPLE WERE ENSLAVED UNDER PHARAOH'S OPPRESSIVE RULE. FEEL THE WEIGHT OF THEIR STRUGGLE, THE CRIES OF THEIR PEOPLE ECHOING IN THE DISTANCE.

EXODUS 2: 1 (NIV)

"AND A MAN OF THE HOUSE OF LEVI WENT AND TOOK AS WIFE A DAUGHTER OF LEVI,"

JACOB & LEAH

STEP INTO THE CAPTIVATING WORLD OF
JACOB AND LEAH, A COUPLE WHOSE STORY
WEAVES TOGETHER THEMES OF LOVE,
SACRIFICE, OBEDIENCE TO GOD, AND THE
PROFOUND COMPLEXITIES OF HUMAN
RELATIONSHIPS. THEIR TALE, SET AGAINST
THE BACKDROP OF ANCIENT CANAAN, IS
ONE OF RESILIENCE, REDEMPTION, AND THE
TRANSFORMATIVE POWER OF ACCEPTANCE.

WITH YOUR COLORING TOOLS IN HAND,
ENVISION THE LANDSCAPES OF LUSH
PASTURES AND ROLLING HILLS. FEEL THE
WARMTH OF THE SUN ON YOUR SKIN AS
YOU IMMERSE YOURSELF IN THE NARRATIVE
OF JACOB, A MAN OF GREAT AMBITION, AND
LEAH, A WOMAN WHOSE HEART LONGED
FOR ACCEPTANCE AND LOVE.

GENESIS 30: 20 (NIV)

"AND LEAH SAID, "GOD HAS ENDOWED ME
WITH A GOOD ENDOWMENT, NOW MY
HUSBAND WILL DWELL WITH ME BECAUSE I
HAVE BORN HIM SIX SONS".

ELKANAH & HANNAH

STEP INTO THE HEARTFELT WORLD OF
ELKANAH AND HANNAH, A COUPLE WHOSE
STORY UNFOLDS AMIDST THE JOYS AND
SORROWS OF LONGING AND ANSWERED
PRAYERS. THEIR TALE IS ONE OF FAITH,
PERSEVERANCE, AND THE TRANSFORMATIVE
POWER OF DEVOTION.

AS YOU TAKE HOLD OF YOUR COLORING
TOOLS, IMAGINE THE ANCIENT CITY OF
RAMATHAIM-ZOPHIM, NESTLED IN THE
HILLS OF EPHRAIM. FEEL THE GENTLE
BREEZE BRUSHING AGAINST YOUR FACE AS
YOU IMMERSE YOURSELF IN THE NARRATIVE
OF ELKANAH, A LOVING HUSBAND, AND
HANNAH, A WOMAN OF PROFOUND FAITH
AND LONGING.

1 SAMUEL 1: 19 (NIV)

"EARLY THE NEXT MORNING THEY AROSE AND
WORSHIPED BEFORE THE LORD AND THEN WENT
BACK TO THEIR HOME AT RAMAH. ELKANAH MADE
LOVE TO HIS WIFE HANNAH, AND THE LORD
REMEMBERED HER."

KING XERXES & ESTHER

STEP INTO THE GRANDEUR AND INTRIGUE OF
THE PERSIAN EMPIRE AS WE DELVE INTO THE
CAPTIVATING STORY OF KING XERXES AND
ESTHER, A COUPLE WHOSE LIVES WERE
ENTWINED IN A TALE OF COURAGE, DESTINY,
AND THE TRIUMPH OF RIGHTEOUSNESS.
THEIRS IS A STORY THAT UNFOLDS AGAINST A
BACKDROP OF OPULENCE, POWER, AND THE
TRANSFORMATIVE IMPACT OF A WOMAN'S
BRAVERY.

AS YOU PICK UP YOUR COLORING TOOLS,
ENVISION THE SPRAWLING PALACES OF
ANCIENT PERSIA, ADORNED WITH ORNATE
DECORATIONS AND FILLED WITH THE
WHISPERS OF COURT POLITICS. FEEL THE
WEIGHT OF RESPONSIBILITY ON KING XERXES'
SHOULDERS AS HE GOVERNS A VAST EMPIRE,
AND THE QUIET STRENGTH THAT EMANATES
FROM ESTHER, A YOUNG JEWISH WOMAN WHO
BECOMES QUEEN.

ESTHER 2: 17 (NIV)

"THE KING LOVED ESTHER MORE THAN ALL THE OTHER
WOMEN, AND SHE OBTAINED GRACE AND FAVOR IN HIS
SIGHT MORE THAN ALL THE VIRGINS; SO HE SET THE
ROYAL CROWN UPON HER HEAD AND MADE HER QUEEN
INSTEAD OF VASHTI."

JOSEPH & ASENATH

STEP INTO THE CAPTIVATING WORLD OF
JOSEPH AND ASENATH, A COUPLE WHOSE
LOVE STORY DEFIED CULTURAL BOUNDARIES
AND TRANSFORMED LIVES. THEIR TALE
UNFOLDS AGAINST THE BACKDROP OF
ANCIENT EGYPT, WHERE DESTINY WEAVED
TOGETHER THE LIVES OF A HEBREW SLAVE
AND AN EGYPTIAN PRINCESS, SHOWCASING
THE POWER OF LOVE, FORGIVENESS, AND
DIVINE PROVIDENCE.

AS YOU GRASP YOUR COLORING TOOLS,
ENVISION THE GRANDEUR OF PHARAOH'S
COURT, ADORNED WITH MAJESTIC
STRUCTURES AND THE WHISPERS OF
INTRIGUE. FEEL THE WARMTH OF THE
EGYPTIAN SUN ON YOUR SKIN AS YOU
IMMERSE YOURSELF IN THE NARRATIVE OF
JOSEPH, A MAN OF INTEGRITY AND WISDOM,
AND ASENATH, A COMPASSIONATE AND
NOBLE-HEARTED PRINCESS.

GENSIS 41:45 (NIV)

"AND PHARAOH CALLED JOSEPH'S NAME ZAPHNATH-
PAANEAH. AND HE GAVE HIM AS A WIFE ASENATH,
THE DAUGHTER OF POTI-PHERAH PRIEST OF ON. SO
JOSEPH WENT OUT OVER ALL THE LAND OF EGYPT. "

HOSEA & GOMER

AS YOU PICK UP YOUR COLORING TOOLS, IMMERSE YOURSELF IN THE WORLD OF ANCIENT ISRAEL, A LAND FILLED WITH SPIRITUAL TURMOIL AND WAYWARD HEARTS. HOSEA, A PROPHET OF GOD, IS COMMANDED TO MARRY GOMER, A WOMAN WHO SYMBOLIZES THE UNFAITHFULNESS OF ISRAEL TO THEIR COVENANT WITH THE ALMIGHTY.

BEGIN BY COLORING IN HOSEA AND GOMER'S INITIAL MEETING, WHERE THE PROPHET'S HEART IS CAPTIVATED BY HER BEAUTY, MIRRORING THE ALLURE OF EARTHLY DESIRES THAT OFTEN LEAD US ASTRAY. LET YOUR COLORS EXPRESS THE PASSION AND DESIRE THAT MARK THE BEGINNING OF THEIR TUMULTUOUS JOURNEY.

HOSEA 1:3 (NIV)

"SO HE MARRIED GOMER DAUGHTER OF DIBLAIM, AND SHE CONCEIVED AND BORE HIM A SON. "

ANANIAS & SAPPHIRA

IN THIS COLORING BOOK, WE EXPLORE THIS
POIGNANT STORY, SET AGAINST THE
BACKDROP OF THE EARLY CHRISTIAN
CHURCH. IMAGINE THE VIBRANT AND
ENTHUSIASTIC COMMUNITY OF BELIEVERS
AS THEY GATHERED TO SUPPORT ONE
ANOTHER AND SHARE THEIR POSSESSIONS,
DRIVEN BY A SENSE OF UNITY AND
DEVOTION.

BEGIN BY COLORING THE SCENE WHERE
ANANIAS AND SAPPHIRA, A MARRIED
COUPLE, MAKE A FATEFUL DECISION TO
SELL A PIECE OF PROPERTY BUT CHOOSE TO
WITHHOLD A PORTION OF THE PROCEEDS
WHILE PRESENTING IT AS THE FULL
AMOUNT TO THE APOSTLES. LET YOUR
COLORS EXPRESS THE SENSE OF SECRECY
AND DECEPTION THAT SHROUDED THEIR
ACTIONS.

ACTS 5:1-2 (NIV)

"NOW A MAN NAMED ANANIAS, TOGETHER WITH HIS
WIFE SAPPHIRA, ALSO SOLD A PIECE OF PROPERTY. 2
WITH HIS WIFE'S FULL KNOWLEDGE HE KEPT BACK
PART OF THE MONEY FOR HIMSELF, BUT BROUGHT
THE REST AND PUT IT AT THE APOSTLES' FEET. "

LAPIDOTH & DEBORAH

LAPIDOTH AND DEBORAH, A REMARKABLE COUPLE FROM THE BIBLE, ARE CELEBRATED FOR THEIR ROLES IN LEADERSHIP, WISDOM, AND COURAGE. IN THIS COLORING BOOK, WE EXPLORE THE CAPTIVATING STORY OF DEBORAH, A PROPHETESS AND JUDGE IN ANCIENT ISRAEL, AND HER SUPPORTIVE HUSBAND, LAPIDOTH, WHO STOOD BY HER SIDE IN THEIR JOURNEY OF FAITH AND LEADERSHIP.

IMAGINE THE SETTING IN ANCIENT ISRAEL, A LAND FILLED WITH CHALLENGES AND CONFLICTS. AS YOU PICK UP YOUR COLORING TOOLS, ENVISION THE COURAGE OF DEBORAH AS SHE SAT UNDER HER PALM TREE, SERVING AS A TRUSTED ADVISOR AND LEADER TO THE PEOPLE OF ISRAEL. LET YOUR COLORS EXPRESS THE WISDOM AND STRENGTH THAT RADIATED FROM HER AS SHE DISPENSED JUSTICE AND GUIDANCE.

JUDGES 4:4 (NIV)

"NOW DEBORAH, A PROPHET, THE WIFE OF LAPPIDOTH, WAS LEADING ISRAEL AT THAT TIME. "

ELIMELECH & NAOMI

ELIMELECH AND NAOMI, A COUPLE FROM
THE BIBLICAL BOOK OF RUTH, EMBODY A
STORY OF LOVE, RESILIENCE, AND THE
ENDURING BONDS OF FAMILY. IN THIS
COLORING BOOK, WE EXPLORE THEIR
JOURNEY, MARKED BY BOTH TRIALS AND
TRIUMPHS, SET AGAINST THE BACKDROP OF
ANCIENT BETHLEHEM.

PICTURE THE TRANQUIL FIELDS OF
BETHLEHEM AS YOU PICK UP YOUR
COLORING TOOLS. FEEL THE WARMTH OF
THE SUN AND THE RUSTLING OF WHEAT IN
THE BREEZE AS YOU IMMERSE YOURSELF IN
THE NARRATIVE OF ELIMELECH, A MAN OF
DEEP FAITH AND RESPONSIBILITY, AND
NAOMI, A DEVOTED WIFE AND MOTHER.

RUTH: 1-2 (NIV)

"THE MAN'S NAME WAS ELIMELECH, AND HIS WIFE
WAS NAOMI. THEIR TWO SONS WERE MAHLON AND
KILION. THEY WERE EPHRATHITES FROM
BETHLEHEM IN THE LAND OF JUDAH".

FELIX & DRUSILLA

THE STORY OF FELIX AND DRUSILLA IS A
CAPTIVATING TALE OF LOVE, AMBITION,
AND THE COMPLEXITIES OF POWER AND
INFLUENCE IN THE ROMAN WORLD. IN THIS
COLORING BOOK, WE DELVE INTO THE
INTRIGUING RELATIONSHIP BETWEEN FELIX,
A ROMAN PROCURATOR, AND DRUSILLA, A
JEWISH PRINCESS.

IMAGINE THE OPULENT SETTING OF THE
ROMAN EMPIRE AS YOU PICK UP YOUR
COLORING TOOLS. ENVISION THE GRANDEUR
OF ROMAN PALACES AND THE BUSTLING
STREETS OF CAESAREA, WHERE FELIX HELD
A POSITION OF AUTHORITY AS PROCURATOR.

ACTS: 24-24 (NIV)

"A FEW DAYS LATER, FELIZ CAME BACK WT H HIS
WIFE DRUSILLA, WHO WAS JEWISH. SENDING FOR
PAUL, THEY LISTENED AS HE TOLD THEM ABOUT
FAITH IN JESUS CHRIST."

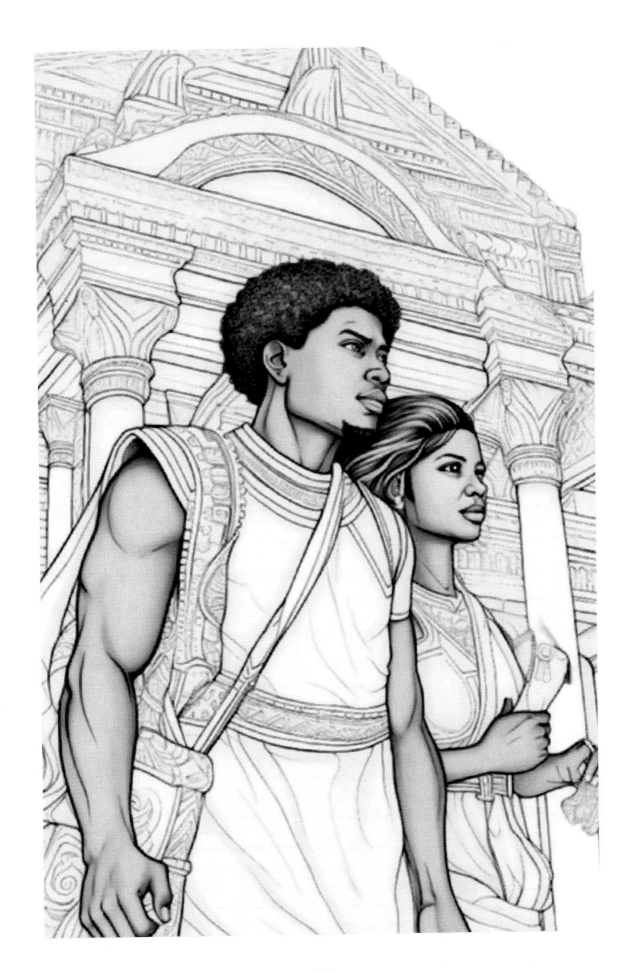

JESUS & THE CHURCH

THE RELATIONSHIP BETWEEN JESUS CHRIST AND THE CHURCH IS AT THE HEART OF CHRISTIAN FAITH AND SPIRITUALITY. IN THIS COLORING BOOK, WE EXPLORE THIS PROFOUND AND ENDURING CONNECTION, REFLECTING ON THE TEACHINGS AND SYMBOLISM ASSOCIATED WITH JESUS AS THE HEAD OF THE CHURCH.

IMAGINE THE SERENE LANDSCAPES OF ANCIENT JUDEA AS YOU PICK UP YOUR COLORING TOOLS. ENVISION THE GATHERINGS OF EARLY CHRISTIANS, SEEKING SPIRITUAL GUIDANCE AND COMMUNITY IN A WORLD MARKED BY DIVERSE BELIEFS AND IDEOLOGIES.

EPHESIANS: 5-25 (NIV)

"FOR HUSBANDS, THIS MEANS LOVE YOUR WIVES, JUST AS CHRIST LOVED THE CHURCH. HE GAVE UP HIS LIFE FOR HER"

MODERN DAY COUPLES

AS WE REACH THE FINAL PAGES OF OUR "BIBLICAL BLACK LOVE" COLORING BOOK, WE REFLECT UPON THE REMARKABLE COUPLES WHOSE STORIES WE'VE EXPLORED. THROUGH VIBRANT COLORS AND INTRICATE STROKES, WE'VE CELEBRATED THE ENDURING LOVE, RESILIENCE, AND FAITH OF THESE COUPLES, BOTH HISTORICAL AND CONTEMPORARY.

FROM THE INSPIRING TALES OF COUPLES LIKE ADAM AND EVE, RUTH AND BOAZ, DEBORAH AND LAPIDOTH, AND SO MANY OTHERS, WE'VE WITNESSED THE BEAUTY OF LOVE GROUNDED IN FAITH AND NOURISHED BY SHARED VALUES. THESE STORIES REMIND US THAT LOVE, WHEN ROOTED IN FAITH AND GUIDED BY PRINCIPLES OF COMPASSION, FORGIVENESS, AND UNITY, CAN OVERCOME ADVERSITY AND FLOURISH.

AS WE CONCLUDE OUR COLORING BOOK, LET THESE STORIES SERVE AS A REMINDER THAT BIBLICAL BLACK LOVE IS A TIMELESS SOURCE OF INSPIRATION. WHETHER YOU'RE IN A LONG-STANDING RELATIONSHIP, A NEW PARTNERSHIP, OR STILL SEEKING LOVE, MAY THESE STORIES REMIND YOU THAT LOVE, WHEN NURTURED WITH FAITH, COMPASSION, AND SHARED VALUES, CAN TRANSCEND TIME AND ADVERSITY, CREATING A LEGACY OF LOVE FOR GENERATIONS TO COME.

ROMANS 12:9-10 (NIV)

"LOVE MUST BE SINCERE. HATE WHAT IS EVIL; CLING TO WHAT IS GOOD. 1BE DEVOTED TO ONE ANOTHER IN LOVE. HONOR ONE ANOTHER ABOVE YOURSELVES."

Biblical Black Love

I WANT TO TAKE A MOMENT TO EXPRESS MY HEARTFELT GRATITUDE TO EACH AND EVERY ONE OF YOU WHO PURCHASED THE "BIBLICAL BLACK LOVE" ADULT COLORING BOOK. YOUR SUPPORT AND ENTHUSIASM FOR THIS PROJECT HAVE BEEN TRULY INSPIRING.

I EMBARKED ON THIS JOURNEY WITH THE INTENTION OF CELEBRATING THE BEAUTY, DIVERSITY, AND RICH CULTURAL HERITAGE REPRESENTED IN BIBLICAL NARRATIVES. I AIMED TO CREATE A SPACE WHERE PEOPLE COULD EXPLORE AND APPRECIATE THE DEPTH OF LOVE AND CONNECTION DEPICTED IN THESE TIMELESS STORIES, WHILE ALSO EMBRACING THE REPRESENTATION OF BLACK LOVE AND EMPOWERMENT.

YOUR DECISION TO BRING THIS COLORING BOOK INTO YOUR LIVES NOT ONLY SUPPORTS MY CREATIVE ENDEAVORS BUT ALSO SIGNIFIES YOUR APPRECIATION FOR DIVERSE REPRESENTATION AND THE CELEBRATION OF LOVE IN ALL ITS FORMS. BY CHOOSING TO ENGAGE WITH THESE ILLUSTRATIONS, YOU CONTRIBUTE TO A MORE INCLUSIVE AND ENRICHED UNDERSTANDING OF HISTORY AND ITS PROFOUND IMPACT ON OUR PRESENT.

I HOPE THAT AS YOU IMMERSE YOURSELF IN THE PAGES OF "BIBLICAL BLACK LOVE," YOU FIND JOY, INSPIRATION, AND MOMENTS OF REFLECTION. MAY THE ACT OF COLORING BECOME A MEDITATIVE AND TRANSFORMATIVE EXPERIENCE, ALLOWING YOU TO CONNECT WITH THE CHARACTERS, STORIES, AND THE INHERENT BEAUTY OF EACH ILLUSTRATION.

ONCE AGAIN, THANK YOU FOR YOUR SUPPORT, FOR EMBRACING DIVERSITY, AND FOR JOINING ME ON THIS MEANINGFUL JOURNEY. I AM HONORED TO HAVE YOU AS PART OF MY COMMUNITY AND LOOK FORWARD TO SHARING MORE CREATIVE ENDEAVORS WITH YOU IN THE FUTURE.

WITH HEARTFELT GRATITUDE,

April La'Prezz

Printed in the United States
by Baker & Taylor Publisher Services

by Baker & Taylor Publisher Services